A glance back at

Coleford

Coleford photographer F.N. Jones took this delightful view showing the town centre, clock tower and market house decorated with a light sprinkling of snow in 1904.

by
Keith & June Webb

Acknowledgements

Thanks for assistance and additional information to Dr. Cyril Hart; Bill Cronin, Conservation Officer, Forest of Dean District Council; the Staff and Students, Wyedean School's World War 1 Victoria Cross Trail; Keith Morgan; Ruth Proctor Hirst; R.G. Shepherd; Roger Carpenter; the late Bill Potter; Members of the Coleford & District WI Market; the Misses F. & C. Pope and other Coleford residents.

A view of Coleford from the Recreation Ground in the 1930s showing the back of the shops, including the Guardian Office in Newland Street and Terrett, Taylor & Son, who sold everything from general ironmongery to house furnishings; they were also agents for agricultural implements, as well as builders, timber and slate merchants.

OTHER TITLES IN THIS SERIES

1. ***A glance back at . . . Lydney*** *by Neil Parkhouse*
2. ***A glance back at . . . Lydney Docks*** *by Neil Parkhouse (due 2001)*
3. ***A glance back at . . . Bream*** *by Ruth Proctor Hirst*
4. ***A glance back at . . . Lydbrook*** *(in preparation)*
5. ***A glance back at . . . Coleford*** *by Keith & June Webb*
6. ***A glance back at . . . Mitcheldean*** *(in preparation)*
7. ***A glance back at . . . Fishing on the Lower Severn*** *(due 2001)*
8. ***A glance back at . . . The Severn Railway Bridge*** *(in preparation)*

Dedicated to the people of Coleford – past, present and its future generations

British Library Cataloguing-in-Publication Data. A catalogue record for this book is available from the British Library

ISBN 0 9533028 8 1

Black Dwarf Publications
47 – 49 High Street, Lydney, Gloucestershire GL15 5DD

Printed by M.D. Jenkins Ltd.,
Unit 53/54, Lydney Trading Estate, Harbour Road, Lydney, Gloucestershire GL15 4EJ

~ A short history of Coleford ~

Coleford lies at the meeting point of ancient routes into the Forest of Dean, between two great river systems, the Severn and Wye. It may not be the geographical centre of the Forest but it is the pulsing heart for local trade in the area. Chepstow, Monmouth and Gloucester form the points of the surrounding triangle. It is the administrative centre, in part, of Forest Enterprise, an agency of the Forestry Commission responsible for the care of the Crown Forests in the greater part of the south western area of the country. The Dean is a prized asset, both for sustainable timber supply and the enjoyment of outdoor recreational pursuits by naturalists, campers, caravanners, canoeists, rockface climbers, walkers and cyclists.

Some of the main timbers in Henry VIII's ship *Mary Rose* came from the Forest of Dean. Later, one of the objectives of the Spanish Armada was to burn the Forest down, to prevent further warships from being built. The 'right kind' of Oaks were only to be found in the Forest for building Shakespeare's recreated theatre, The Globe, in London in the 1990s, whilst the main bowsprit of Brunel's *S.S. Great Britain*, in Bristol, has been replaced by means of a single piece of timber, cut and shaped from an individual Dean Forest tree.

The lower reaches of the Severn bound the Forest plateau to the east and the Wye on the west. Mammoths and hippopotami roamed the Wye Valley before the dawn of known history. It was an area very much cut off from time, until the coming of the motorways and the first Severn Road Bridge. 'Twixt Severn and Wye' is an impressive and attractive description for an area of outstanding natural beauty. On the other hand, a well-kept secret during the Second World War was that the Forest was used for the biggest reserve of ammunition – a stockpile amassed for the assault on Occupied Europe. The residents of Coleford too, played their part in both World Wars.

The first settlers in Coleford would have been attracted by the confluence of its three streams, a ford, abundant land for agricultural crops and grazing, a plentiful supply of iron ore and, of course, wood. In their turn, the Romans knew the area well, the iron deposits, to be smelted and made into weapons, attracting them too. In Medieval times, the region was the greatest iron working area in the country. There are ancient iron mines, called The Scowles, near Coleford. They are now clothed in nature's vegetation, giving them a sense of mystery as you explore. The three streams, Col Brook, Thurston's Brook and Sluts Brook, have since been culverted or diverted to by-pass the town centre, to obviate flooding. By the 18th century most of the land around Coleford was cultivated by tenant farmers.

Coleford is not mentioned in the Domesday Book (1086). It would then have been part of the King's forest. The name was Colevorde in 1275 and in 1710 there were 160 houses. Today the older town's centre is a conservation area of buildings, which together have architectural merit.

During Victorian and Edwardian times, Coleford was a hive of small shops, offices, business premises and countless public houses. Some of the town's better buildings were originally hotels or hostelries, as the distance which could be travelled in a day in times past, usually meant an overnight stopover was required when doing business or visiting in the area. Much later it even boasted two railway stations, belonging to rival railway companies.

The Severn & Wye Railway Company's station opened first, in 1875. The Coleford Railway Company commenced running to the town in 1883, the first train arriving just before 9 am to be greeted by a large cheering crowd. The supposed fertility rite of throwing rice over the first departing train evidently did not have the desired effect, however. Within a year the line had been taken over by the Great Western Railway and it was an early closure casualty, services ceasing on New Year's Day 1917. In 1894, the Severn & Wye & Severn Bridge Railway, as it had become by then, was jointly taken over by the Midland and Great Western Railway companies, as neither was prepared to give way to the other in an area of potentially lucrative mineral wealth.

Today, all the deep coal mines in Dean have long since closed and the costs of extraction do not make exploitation of the large reserves still underlying the Forest an economically viable proposition. However, an increase in commercial demand and a scarcity of materials obtained from elsewhere could change the value and demands for the Forest's resources overnight. Indeed, many of the sites of natural beauty were originally of man made origin, which nature has reclothed after abandonment.

The designated Conservation area radiates out from around the Church Tower on the Tump, which was the town's Market Place. Following the granting of a Market Charter in 1661, there were regular scenes of sheep sales and fairs, with stalls selling such delights as roly-poly puddings, gingersnaps, and faggots and peas, alongside the helter-skelters, gallopers and roundabouts. Pens were set up on the impacted earthen carriageway and larger animals were tethered nearby.

The old Church Tower has an embattled parapet, with pinnacles as the continuation of stepped diagonal buttresses and clock faces on the south, west and north sides. Here stood a chapel from at least as early as 1489, which was enlarged in 1743 and replaced by a larger octagonal chapel in 1821. This was subsequently demolished in 1882, leaving only the tower and a memorial cross built on the site of the altar. The weather vane atop the tower is a silhouette of the Forest Miner emblem. He carries a candle in a holder clamped between his teeth and a hod on his back. The nearby water trough was provided in 1897 to commemorate the 60th year of the reign of Queen Victoria. It is topped by some decorative wrought ironwork, forged in Coalbrookdale. In the past, it was occasionally used to dowse unruly drunkards, thrown out of one of the town's many public houses.

On a quiet afternoon in the early 1930s, local children gather to watch Cinderford-based photographer R.G. Gibbs as he takes this postcard view of Coleford's town centre and the old church tower.

A few paces to the north stood, in 1608, a preaching cross and, a little later, a Market Hall, which was damaged during the Civil War in 1643. It was rebuilt in 1691 and later it was also used as the Town Hall. During the Second World War, the building was extensively used by the U.S. Army and Joe Louis, the renowned World Heavyweight Champion boxer, once paid a fleeting visit to it while on a morale boosting tour for American troops in the area. Sadly, the building was demolished in 1968 – a decision very much regretted today.

Looking above the shopfronts reveals the old Coleford – the varied styles of architecture, the pitches of the roofs and the Georgian fronts, some partially concealed under rendering and plaster. From this, it can be imagined how the town would have looked when most of the buildings were private dwellings, the streets and Tump unsurfaced, and muddy or red with iron ore dust, according to the season. On the east side of the Market Place is a row of five shops, the fronts of which cannot hide their former glory as Georgian houses. They vary in styles and roof types but all blend harmoniously.

The traffic has been reduced by diverting some of it away. This has made the area more pedestrian friendly, with pavias where animal stalls once stood. The passageway metal arch facing onto the Tump, which commemorates the famed Mushets of the town, leads through into a large modern tree-lined car park, with other shops and a Health Centre where once stood the town's two stations, their attendant buildings and the Coal Merchants yards. The former GWR Goods Shed is now a Railway Museum; it was opened in 1988 by former Forest railwayman Mike Rees, who saved it from demolition literally at the eleventh hour, and contains many items of local interest.

The nearby modern Fire Station on Cinder Hill represents a proud commitment, going back to 1868, when a volunteer brigade was formed to man a fire engine brought from Gloucester by an insurance company. The stirring sight of a hand-operated fire pump, drawn by galloping horses, speeding its way to a fire in the town can be well imagined. The present day Fire Service was formed in 1931, becoming part of the Gloucestershire Fire & Rescue Service in 1948. It is still manned by trained volunteers.

Almost opposite is Forest House Hotel, formerly known as Tump House. In 1810, it was leased by David Mushet, a pioneer in the development of the iron industry. Originally born in Scotland, he came to Coleford from Derbyshire to take over the running of Whitecliff Furnace and then built his Darkhill Ironworks at Gorsty Knoll. His son, Robert Forester Mushet, was born at Tump House and it was he who later perfected the Bessemer process for the large scale production of steel. He made its production both reliable and economically practicable, having found solutions to the problems before others had even fully understood the process involved. Robert was farsighted and also developed the first self-hardening tool steel, a forerunner of all high-speed steel alloys. A plaque has been erected on Forest House to record the period of the Mushets' residence there. Nearby, in Mushet Place, there is another metal plaque recording the site of a barn, where many of their earlier experiments were carried out.

Beside the Forest of Dean District Council Offices, built in 1989, is Lawnstone House, one of the largest houses in the town. This was The Lawnstone Family & Commercial Hotel in the 19th century, until it closed in 1889. It is now an annexe to the council offices. The Cinema was built in 1906 as a drill hall for the Coleford Volunteers. Shortly afterwards, the Colour-Sergeant began free Magic Lantern shows. This was followed by the era of variety acts and silent films. It is now a first-class modern, comfortable cinema, showing two film programmes simultaneously. The car showroom next door was originally the Bristol Carriage Company (later Bristol Bus Company) depot. Previously, George Mowbray had his saddlers here and Mr. Green's shoemakers shop occupied the site.

On both sides of this street many of the buildings are listed as having Special Architectural or Historic Interest. All the buildings on the right, below the former Post Office, are late 18th century or earlier. Opposite there is a terrace of three Georgian houses, with delightful traceried fanlights, original doorways and a stone apron with only the remains of iron railings. They were removed during the Second World War '*for the War Effort*', this being the explanation given as they were taken away (everywhere in the country suffered such desecration of its local ironwork, damage which has now been largely proved a waste as most of the metal so gathered was useless and thrown away – it was really a means of motivating the population). The next house along was, for many years, the Waverley Temperance Hotel and it still retains its two fine round-headed projecting doorcases, with panelling and fluted architraves.

On the lower side of the Tump is the Angel Hotel. An inn has stood here since 1608 and served many purposes besides being an alehouse. In the 18th century it was also the Excise Office and Post Office. Around 1810 'old Mousell' was the local postman, who could neither read nor write, so one wonders how the correspondence ever reached those for whom it was intended. It was a coaching inn on the routes between Monmouth, Gloucester and Bristol. The carriage arch and yard can still be seen but it is now glassed in and carpeted for use as a bar. On the front of the building is a plaque commemorating Warren James, the leader of the rioters of 1831, who tore down the Forest inclosures which had been made by the Crown to protect the growing trees. These had excluded the horses, sheep, cattle and pigs that, since time out of mind, had grazed the Forest by custom. The rebellion was an attempt to protect their traditional way of life from the threat of increasing outside interference. Warren James was captured and brought to the Angel, before being tried at the Quarter Sessions in Gloucester. He was found guilty and transported to Tasmania. Although later pardoned, he had no money to return to his beloved Forest and died out there, aged only 49.

The nearby Old White Hart public house, at the beginning of St. Johns Street, is one of the oldest surviving buildings. It dates from the 17th century, when it was a brew house. Other buildings in the street are in their original condition, but are being sensitively restored. On one side is an archway into the old Wine and Spirits Vault. In the early part of the 20th century it was owned by J. W. Watts Esq., who also owned the Waverley Temperance Hotel in the High Street. The one may have required the other but to profit from both appears to be conflicting interests!

At the traffic lights in the centre of the town can be seen the post war-style Police Station and adjacent to the car park is where once stood the home of Captain Angus Buchanan VC. Also beside the traffic lights, on the opposite corner, stands the Kings Head public house. During the Civil War (1643-9), Coleford stood for the Parliamentarians, mainly because of damage done to the woods by Sir John Wintour of Lydney, who had been granted the Dean's timber by King Charles I. A troop of two thousand soldiers, commanded by Major-General Lawdey, was dispatched from Monmouth to assist in the siege of Gloucester. While in Coleford it is said that they barricaded a mansion and the old market house was burned. In retaliation, Major-General Lawdey was shot with a silver bullet from the window of a house that used to stand on this site.

A short way along Gloucester Road from the traffic lights is Poolway House, a 16th and 17th century guesthouse and restaurant. As the Civil War progressed, Coleford changed its allegiance to the Crown and tradition has it that Colonel Morgan E. Worgan, then owner of Poolway House, saved the life of King Charles I at the battle of Edge Hill. For this deed he was granted three boons; that he might have the highest pew in the Church of Newland, that his tenants and neighbours might brew and sell beer unmolested and that he might have a pup out of the Queen's bitch 'Lily'. Opposite, there is a lane leading to an ancient hollow way to Wynols Hill. In 1331 there is a reference to '*The King's highway from la Wynholt towards le Coleforde*'.

Between the King's Head and the Forest Enterprise buildings is an uneven lane, which belies its importance to the everyday history of the town. Tucked in a corner is the remains of what was called 'The Spout'. It was here that the residents and their children congregated every day to get water for their daily needs. This was the town's main water supply. From 1873 the Board of Health supplemented this supply by means of a water cart, bought by local subscription. The upper part of the town did not get piped water until 1932. For many years, strategically located nearby was the local children's favourite sweet shop – 'Zake Benfield's round by the Spout' – where a penny's pocket money would purchase four ounces of sweets.

Unfortunately, the Spout was located beside what was then the open Thurstan's Brook.

As there were no sanitation services in Coleford, the brooks were used to carry away the town's effluent. Pollution increased as the water flow dwindled and remained a nuisance until the middle of the 20th century. Between 1931-5, the Urban District Council built sewers to replace the surface gutters but a full system for the town, including a treatment works, did not come until the 1950s. If anyone was missing for a while, they were said to be probably 'up the spout!' There is very little of the Spout left now but it would be tragic for it to be lost altogether, without trace, like so much else. It represents an aspect of the social history of the real people of Coleford. If it disappears, will future generations ask why we did not care enough to ensure its preservation?

Forest Enterprise, an Agency of the Forestry Commission, is to be found in Bank House, a late 18th century building in the classical style, with a decorative 19th century wooden trellis porch and a circular traceried window above. It has been sympathetically enlarged and the woodlands of the Dean are now managed from here. It also houses the

Coleford 'Buffs' church parade with Coleford Town Band, August 1952. The Town Band was formed by 1860 and gave its last concert around 1995. The parade is passing Barter's fruit and veg shop; Mrs Barter can be seen watching their passage through one of the upper windows.

office of the Deputy Gaveller who, on behalf of the Crown, administers the granting of gales to Forest Freeminers. Any adult male who has been born in the Hundred of St. Briavels and who has worked in a mine for a year and a day can claim the privilege, upon representation to the Deputy Gaveller. Thus the closure of the local maternity unit on economic grounds has caused consternation. Freehold property owners in the Forest of Dean do not own the mineral rights under their land; they belong to the Crown.

There was a circulating library in the town in the 1840s. A Mechanical Institute was formed in 1855, with a reading room and library, but this closed in the early 1860s. By 1863 Coleford had a privately owned reading room and later, in the 1930s, a library was run from a stationers shop. In 1959 the County Library, which had been situated in Cinder Hill, was housed in a former chapel in the High Street. It moved to its present building, adjacent to Bank House, in 1964. Beyond the library is the former Independent Congregational Chapel, with the date 1842 on its projecting two-column Doric porch. It has now been converted to apartments but, during the Second World War, the local community used the building for many events held in aid of the 'War Effort'.

On the other corner of Bank Street and St. John Street, now redeveloped, is the site of a house where Lady Healey, nee Edna Edmunds (wife of the Life Peer) was born and lived until she went up to Oxford University. She was described by her primary school head-teacher as the brightest pupil she had ever had! Beside the shop on the corner there is a narrow lane. It was the course of the 1812 Tramway from Monmouth to the coal mines beyond Coleford. It also served the Boxbush Iron-ore Pit, which has now been built over. The route of the 'Dramroad' (as known locally) can be easily followed beyond the town and the former Great Western Railway branch followed largely the same valley route down towards the River Wye.

Newland Street runs off the Market Square too. There are some interesting buildings here, as well. Look up a narrow passage at the beginning of the street and you will see a stone building, which was once the stable of the Waverley Hotel. After having been derelict for some time it has now been made habitable again. Believe it or not, it has previously served as the library and a child health clinic. The imposing building beside the passage and before the public toilets is Caragh House. Its rendered walls cannot hide the fact that it is a good example of an 18th century grand scale classical town house. It has a central 6-panel door with pedimented wooden doorcase and original lion doorknocker. This entrance is now closed and the steps and railings have been removed. In the early 19th century it belonged to James Teague, an Industrialist, who built the first tramroad in Gloucestershire. He was also a shareholder in the Whitecliff Furnace, which is much further down Newland Street, out of the town.

On the right-hand side of the road there are late 18th century Grade II Listed buildings. One of the shops has oriel windows above, whilst others have reeded stone architraves, carved decorations, a round arched doorway and windows between four thin iron columns, with decorated capitals giving them a quiet dignity. In 1831 a printing press was set up behind these shops. One became the office of the *Dean Forest Guardian*, a newspaper started in 1874. It was printed elsewhere after 1922. Upon amalgamation with two other newspapers it became *The Forester* in 1991 and although recently taken over by a Gloucestershire newspaper group, its Forest traditions have been assured.

Beside the railway bridge that spans the road is the old Gas Works, opened in 1840 to produce gas for the town, plus coke and tar. The Gas Works closed in 1946 and its gasholders were demolished in 1974. The West Gloucestershire Power Company brought electricity to Coleford in 1924. The workmanship of the single span skew bridge of brick on stone pillars is superb. It carried the Great Western line into the town from Monmouth. The cottages just beyond the bridge were built for the Station Master and railway employees. After the line from Monmouth was closed to the west of Whitecliff Quarry in 1917, stone went out by rail via Coleford on the Severn & Wye line to Parkend and Lydney. When the GWR rails were taken up they were requisitioned and re-laid in France, to aid the supply of ammunition for the massive artillery bombardments then taking place at the Front.

Down the road, lie several buildings with interesting histories, such as Mill House. In the 19th century this was William Stenson's steam mill, engine house and home. He came to Coleford in 1809 to work for David Mushet and was described as a first rate engineer and mineralogist. His son married the niece of George Stephenson, the famous railway engineer. Further on is Whitecliff House, built in the late 16th century and enlarged in 1790. In 1816 James Teague bought it and spent considerable funds on enlarging it. It was described as '*a mansion, most noble and grand and beautiful. It is a most healthy spot to live.*' Sadly Teague did not live to confirm this as he died before he could take up residence. Many of the Teague family influenced the industrial history of the area in their time.

Whitecliff Furnace, which was built about 1800, was an early coke-fuelled blast furnace for making iron. Before it was completed deep snow fell and such heavy rains followed that the brook flooded, and in one night the partly constructed furnace was swept away. The original shareholders retired from the project, and James Teague and others took over the construction. Members of the Whitecliff Furnace Trust in the early 1970s extensively repaired the remnants of the furnace, as part of a comprehensive conservation plan that has yet to be completed. The site is now under the guardianship of the Dean Heritage Trust Museum.

Dominating the town, on the hillside above is Coleford's Parish church, Saint John the Evangelist. However, Coleford is lucky that the church is still standing. It is alleged that the manager of the Gas Works went into a corridor below the East End of the church with a lighted candle to find a gas leak! Mr. Harold Bright, who was then a churchwarden, witnessed the resultant blackened beams over 50 years ago.

After World War Two the Government set up the Royal Forest of Dean Development Association, to deliberately encourage businesses and industry to come into the area. This was to replace the jobs being lost in the mining and quarrying industry. So began the biggest social upheaval in the area during modern times. Also, as a larger proportion of the country's population grows older, because we live longer, many 'outsiders' have come into this beautiful area to retire. Nature has now reclaimed the ravaged former industrial landscape.

The nearby Bells Golf Club and Hotel, in Lords Hill, was the onetime Bells Grammar School. Built in 1875, it served as the Grammar School until the early 1970s. Dennis Potter, the prominent playwright, was a pupil there. His memories of his early Forest life enriched his work and marked him out as one of the most outstanding writers of our time. Part of the golf course had been a site of opencast coal mining, before reclamation and landscaping was carried out.

The whole area will not be unique, in cultural terms, for much longer, as the outside world's standards, pressures and practices, which are insidiously implanted via the media on the expectations of the next generation of Foresters and newcomers, have their inevitable influence. It is almost a moment too late to take a glance back at the Coleford of yesteryear but here we have a singular opportunity to do so through this collection of old photographs, postcards and the memories of local people.

Coleford's first photographer was John Porter, who was taking pictures by 1883 at least. This group was taken by him at Coleford vicarage on 14 July 1904, although what the occasion was is not known. A Miss Brice is seated in the centre of the front row (white blouse), alongside her hatless clergyman brother. The postcard was sent in August 1904 to Tom Oldland, an ex-Colefordian who had emigrated to Toronto in Canada.

F. N. JONES,
COLEFORD
THE RISING GENERATION
OF THE FOREST OF DEAN

The shop of F.N. Jones, portrait and postcard photographer, at 8 Gloucester Road. In the first quarter of the 20th century Jones published a large range of postcard views of the town and surrounding area, including outlying villages such as Milkwall and Bream. One of his best known cards (and most sought after by collectors) was the superb collage of local children's portraits entitled '*The Rising Generation of the Forest of Dean*', illustrated left. He was also responsible for the evocative snow scene, below, looking down the High Street towards the clock tower in about 1905. The studio in Gloucester Road, pictured above about 1908, is still open today and is now run by his son.

Coleford was a chapel of ease to the Parish of Newland, which had been endowed by Queen Anne, but its upkeep appears to have been solely by public subscription. The old church was pulled down in 1820 and replaced by one with an octagonal shape because of the restricted space. It was similar to the church at Parkend. It was replaced in 1880 by St. Johns Church in Boxbush Hill, the old church having become too small for its growing congregation; it was demolished two years later.

The town centre and church tower around 1900 with the Waverley Hotel on the left. In later years, Fred Hose practised dentistry next door. He had a reputation for being quite forceful with stubborn teeth that he thought should come out. The tall chimney on Mr Hose's house collapsed during a storm one night about 1950 and went through the roof of the adjacent shop, which is now 'The Crusty Loaf' bakers. There are railings around the tower and in front of The Waverley and Bristol Terrace. These were removed during the Second World War as part of the War Effort.

A view down the High Street in the 1950s, with the Bristol Omnibus Co's transport garage on the left. Latterly, the garage was a Ford dealership, Wyedean Motors, and is now Wyedean Car Sales, part of the Watts group. Beyond is the Georgian period Bristol Terrace. George Mobury, a saddler, and Mrs Horwood, a dressmaker, had premises near the Waverley.

Despite its ancient appearance, the cross had only been erected some 20 years previously when this picture was taken by Coleford photographer John Porter in the early 1900s. It marks the site of the altar of the old chapel, demolished in 1882. The Forest of Dean District Council had plans to move it in early proposals to redesign the Tump area to help traffic flow, but public opinion prevailed and the Cross remained. The revised plans took this into account and part pedestrianisation and re-routing of some traffic was completed in 1999. Trotters Ltd, Gents & Ladies Outfitters & Milliners, is to the right of the cross. They finally closed in the 1990s and the loss was much lamented.

A busy Market Place around 1925, with delivery vans, carts and buses much in evidence (the message on the back of the postcard is rather good – it reads '*Arrived safely. Just off to see a few friends. Men friends of course.*' Perhaps wisely, it is just signed 'J'!). There were market stalls at the Town Hall on Fridays and Saturdays, not only for clothing but cobblers attended too. They could repair any footwear including the hobnailed boots that were much favoured for working in the pits. Here, on Fridays, old Mrs Padmore sold home-made sweets at fourpence a pound and Walter Hughes sold fish. The Hall was the venue for 'Flitch Trials', even as late as the 1950s. A 'Judge' would be appointed to oversee the proceedings and Councils for the Prosecution and Defence were chosen. They would all be suitably attired in Court dress, including wigs and gowns. The trials were a popular form of entertainment in the Forest, couples competing for a flitch of bacon. Their claim that they had not quarrelled for a year and a day would be rigorously tested and witnesses could be called to support or challenge the claims. It could be seen as tempting fate, leading to arguments at the trial or for 'skeletons in the cupboard' being unwittingly exposed. Coleford was granted a Market Charter in 1661. It used to have a cattle market on the last Friday of every month and fairs twice a year, on 20 June and 24 November, for the sale of cattle, cheese and wool. During the Great War of 1914 – 1918 it was the venue for Army Recruiting drives at which large crowds gathered. The building became more familiarly known as the Town Hall in the early part of the 20th century. The similar view on the right was taken in the 1940s, with Staits bicycle shop (owned by Richard 'Dickie' Staits) and Mills gents outfitters on the right, and Barters grocers behind the wall, left. During WW2 many children came to Coleford as evacuees, due to the bombing of major cities like Bristol. Upon arrival the children were first taken to the Town Hall, to await their selection by Forest families prepared to take them. Although home-sick, being away from home for the first time, the warmth of the Forest's close knit families must have gone a long way towards making their stay memorable.

The Forest of Dean Volunteers (Her Majesty's Forest of Dean Rifle Corps) was founded in 1859 and 'G' Coleford Company was part of it. They held drills in the Market Hall, rifle practice at Wimberry Rifle Range and they also formed their own band. It is thought this 1880s photograph shows the Rifle Volunteer Band (the uniforms are very military in style and the banner shows men in the early Corps uniform), but what the occasion was is not known.

Celebrations in the Market Place in June 1911 for the coronation of King George V. Note Trotters shop with the windows boarded for protection, whilst the Trotter family watch proceedings from the balcony. The large banner on the left belongs to Coleford Baptist Sunday School and a glance at the picture will give an indication of why milleners did such good business at this time!

Territorials parading beside the Town Hall. This is a drill but most of these men were soon to go off and fight in the First World War. Many did not return. The Territorials succeeded the Volunteers whose instructor, Colour Sergeant Richard Reeves, inspired the building of the Drill Hall, which later housed the Studio Cinema. The photograph was taken by John Porter around 1910.

The bottom of High Street as seen from the Market Place in the early 1930s. No traffic problems at this time with only one car and a couple of motor cycles on view. The two men on the left stand in the doorway of Trotters shop, watching the photographer at work. Note the WW1 cannon displayed by the clock tower; like the railings, it went for the 'War Effort' in WW2.

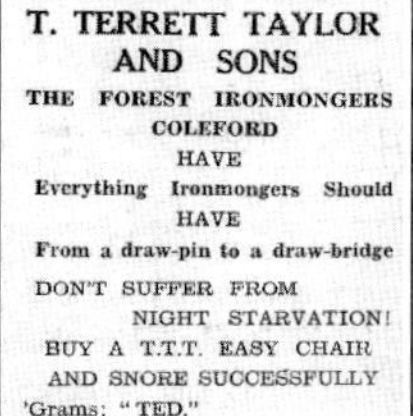

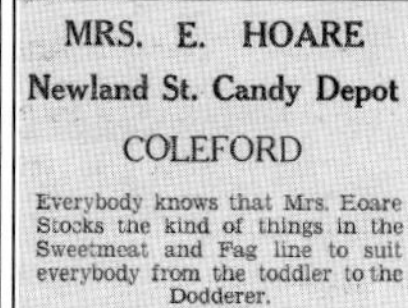

Adverts by various well known Coleford businesses, from guide books between 1905 and 1940. Hornby trains from Watts' Library, postcards from Arthur Bright and Bass ales from John Watts, whilst Hatton's could sell you a motor car, a bicycle, a sewing machine, a musical instrument or a gun!

Arthur T. Bright

CROWN PRINTER AND STATIONER

Coleford : : : Glos.

LARGE STOCK OF PHOTOCROM CO.'S FRAMED VIEWS OF THE FOREST OF DEAN AND WYE VALLEY.

Best Selection of Coloured Pictorial Post-Cards in the District.

Proprietor of "THE DEAN FOREST GUARDIAN," the Advertiser for the Forest and Neighbouring Towns, and by far the most widely-circulated Newspaper in West Gloucestershire.

HATTON'S

Cycle & Motor Works

COLEFORD, GLOS.,

For the Best Value in

CYCLES, MOTOR CYCLES AND CARS.

Agent for all the Best Makes in above.

Repairs and Vulcanizing a Speciality.

Makers of the Forester Cycles and Motors.

Garage, Petrol, Greases and Oils, Etc.

Cycle Accessories in great variety.

Sewing Machines, Mail Carts. Gun, Rifles and Ammunition. Musical Instruments and Athletic Goods of all Description.

A close up view of the Waverley Temperance Hotel. In the 1820s it was owned by Dr Jennings, who died in 1893. It was then bought by John Watts, who rented it to Jack Mansfield. His son Bob, later to become Vicar of Newnham, was born there. In 1915 it was rented to Benjamin Arthur Pope at £35 per annum and it was later bought by Mr & Mrs Pope, at auction, in 1921. The Pope family lived there until 1975. It is said that when John Watts died more than half Coleford was up for sale. The auction was held at the Angel Hotel on 21 August 1921. Amongst the other properties auctioned were the Red Lion and White Swan public houses, the Unicorn Hotel, shop properties including 14 Market Place (rented by Williams, Cotton & Co) and 1 St. John Street (wine & spirit merchants), and Rose Bank, a dwelling house with garden in Cinder Hill.

Part of Market Place and the top of Newland Street, photographed in the early 1930s by R.G. Gibbs. Newland Street actually begins at the white house just past the corner on the left and the other side of the sunblinds on the right. The shops include the India & China Tea Co, the London Central Meat Co (always known by the locals as 'The Foreign Butchers'), Bolters hair dressers & tobacconists, founded in 1818, Williams & Cotton's grocers (noted in the auction details above) and Watts Book Shop. The Bolter's ad (right) is from a 1937 Coleford Carnival brochure.

A spectacular view of Newland Street from the top of the clock tower, taken in 1951 with work underway on installing the new main sewer. It is difficult to believe now that, up until this late date, the Whitecliff Brook was an open sewer. On the right is Yates's newsagents, where you could also book tickets for the Red & White buses. The Baptist Chapel and its rather overgrown cemetery can be seen at the top of the view. In 1971, the old Baptist Sunday School on the corner of Bowens Hill was made into three apartments. Opposite the schoolrooms, about 1919, Coleford's first garage, with petrol pumps outside, was opened by Messrs Watts Factors but it was soon taken over by Charles Higgs and Layton Niblett. It is remembered for the constant pervading smell of engine fumes.

The works in Newland Street looking back towards the clock tower, with local children inspecting progress. The street flooded regularly, whenever it rained heavily, an occurrence which can only have been made worse by the sewage in the Whitecliff Brook. The fast flowing torrent which resulted would come up to the top of the steps. Parts of the centre still have a tendency to flood now, despite the town's elevation.

The first Baptist meeting house and dwelling for the Minister was acquired in 1805 for £40. The present Baptist Church, left, was built in l858 and the facade is said to resemble the front of the Cathedral of Amiens. When built it had no organ, until a second hand one was purchased from Leeds Town Hall in the early 1870s. The facilities were extended in 1889, when the congregation had increased to over 300. In the early 1970s, Phoenix Court was built in front of the old graveyard to fund the modernisation of the church. Services today are held on the first floor of the chapel whilst the ground floor houses the Sunday School room.

Newland Street with, on the left hand side the Baptist Chapel, Mrs Frowes's cottage and the British School Rooms. On the right is the Rag and Bone Store, known for its whalebone over the doorway – a sight that always impressed the local children. An exotic activity carried on in this street was the making of silk during the 19th century. The building beyond the steps on the right is Huntington House. Built in 1790 and now modernised, it was once a Chapel of the Countess of Huntingdon's Connection, a Calvinistic Methodist Church. It later became a Church of England Infants School and a home for 'disadvantaged females'.

Two views from Market Place towards Newland Street, top circa 1900 and below in the 1940s. The man with the wheelbarrow in the top picture may have come with building materials from Terrett Taylor & Sons. Note Horwood's Hotel beyond him – is this the Horwood who later took over the Lawnstone Hotel? Caragh House is the dominant building in the centre of the picture at the beginning of Newland Street. James Teague, who was involved in the Whitecliff furnace much further down the road, owned it in 1817. Later the Porter Family lived here. Ambrose Porter became organist at Lichfield Cathedral. More recently the property was owned by the late Baden Watkins, son of the Founder of Fred Watkins Engineers not far out of the town at Sling. Previous to the house being built the White Horse Inn and a Blacksmiths stood there. The small building beyond was the rates office, with a staff of two.

Provis & Horwood

MARKET PLACE,
And Opposite the Bank,

Coleford, GLOS.

Family Drapers,
Silk Mercers,
Milliners and
Ladies' Outfitters

CARPETS, RUGS,
FLOOR CLOTHS.

Provis & Horwood (previously Provis Bros), milliners, drapers and fabrics. Walter Provis acted as an Insurance Agent in the town for fire insurance and life assurance. He took pride in being a Shipping Agent as well as also being the representative for the National Freehold Land Society and the British Land Company Ltd. This advertisement showing the front of their store is from around 1910.

It is likely that the two pictures on this page, along with the other 1940s views shown, were taken during or shortly after WW2. Note the two men chatting above (by the moped) who are in uniform and the black and white striped signposts in the pictures, painted so to aid visibility during the blackout. This photograph is looking at the Market Place from the top of Newland Street.

The entrance to St. John's Street from the Market Place. The drinking trough was built to commemorate Queen Victoria's Diamond Jubilee. Complete with gas lamp and built of grey Forest stone, it was declared 'open' at a ceremony on 10 November 1898. Note the red & white bus waiting outside Chas. Key's general store. Despite its stripes the handsome signpost blends far more with its surroundings than do the enormous metal boards provided for today's motorists.

This 1920s postcard shows the newly built Lloyds Bank, now Lloyd's TSB and a Listed polygonal 20th century building. Also prominent in the picture is a Hereford Transport bus; the crew have climbed out to pose for photographer F.N. Jones whilst waiting for departure time, probably on a service to Ross. Behind the bus can be seen the front of the Angel Hotel.

Two contrasting views looking towards the Kings Head. J.T. William's wine store and chemists appears on the corner of Market Place and St. John's Street in the upper view. It was demolished to make way for the new Lloyd's Bank premises.. The Angel Hotel board, hanging from a wooden rail between it and the Market Hall, was very much a feature of the coaching era. This picture has been published several times before but it has the appearance of a very early photograph, much earlier than previously credited. The Market Hall was reconstructed in 1867 and the arches were filled in; the picture appears to have been taken before that work was carried out, which would date it as mid 1860s at least, making it one of the earliest surviving photographs of the town. The men's clothing would also support this date. The view below shows the same scene in the early 1930s.

Looking towards the Kings Head public house from the Market Place, circa 1900. Provis Bros., on the left, had been trading in the town as drapers and grocers since at least the early 1880s and, as seen previously, later became Provis & Howood. Barton & Barnard's pharmacy is on the corner; it was also the opticians and sold 'Animal Medicines' veterinary products as well.

Gloucester Road as it appeared around 1910. Coleford's first police station was established here at No. 3 by 1849 at least. Whilst the right hand side of the road has changed completely from this view, the opposite side is still remarkably intact and with an array of interesting small shops.

Looking towards the clock tower from St. John's Street, originally named Birmingham Street; no doubt the name was changed in the 1880s when the new church was built. The cottage at the rear of the Angel Hotel became Miss Kathleen Miller's sweet shop – the building does look something like a 'Ginger Bread House'. The street surface is muddy and unsurfaced in this circa 1900 view.

St. John's Street in the 1940s, with Miss Miller's sweet shop, by now a tobacconists, at the far end. Beyond the hardware shop were, for many years South Herefordshire Agricultural Cornmerchants, known by all as 'Shacs'; they closed in the late 1980s. Also in this street was G.B. Kilminster, boot dealer, who proudly proclaimed 'Quality high, prices low', whilst between the wars Angus Buchanan V.C., solicitor, had his offices in this street too. Following the recent town centre improvements and alterations to traffic flow, St. John's is now a one way street, taking traffic out of Coleford.

Although this circa 1910 postcard of St. John's Street is captioned Church Street, there is no evidence that it was ever named this. Pont & Adams, grocery and provisions store, is on the right. It was renowned for the home-cured bacon at eight pence per pound. All the shop fronts were festooned with the products they were selling and window displays were piled high in an attempt to attract customers into one shop in preference to any other. Further down on the right is the White Swan owned by John Watts and rented by Miss Mary Fox for £16 per annum. The Monmouth Tramroad formerly ran down the lane to the right in the foreground. On the left is The Forester, coffee tavern and commercial hotel. Today, in premises just beyond it can be found The Forest Bookshop, where you may have purchased this book.

Another evocative 1940s view, looking towards St. John's Street and the centre from Sparrow Hill. The pub round the corner to the right was called the Masons Arms. It has reverted to its original name of 'Help Me Through the World' but how is uncertain because it is no longer a public house.

A circa 1930 aerial view of the centre of Coleford, with Newland Street bottom right and St. John's Street bottom left. Also shown are the two railway stations. Because of the rivalry involved at the time they were built in the 1870s/80s, there was no direct rail connection between the two lines. After 1916, trains to and from Whitecliff Quarry had to perform a complicated double reverse shunt manoeuvre through the sidings. This odd situation was not resolved until the early 1950s.

Two views of the Severn & Wye station at Coleford in its later years. Opened in 1875, it closed to passengers in 1929 when the GW and LMS Joint Committee withdrew all the passenger services north of Lydney. The railcar in the picture above was visiting on a railtour in 1950. The brick built station building was a replacement for the wooden one burnt down in 1918. The view below, taken in 1958, shows almost the full extent of the station, with the timber built S & W goods shed in the background. If stood in this spot today, you would be looking along the front of the Pyatt's Court shopping development towards the Co-op store, recently taken over from Somerfields.

The GWR's branch from Monmouth opened in 1883 but was not a success and the station closed to passengers in 1916, although a stub to Whitecliff remained to serve the quarry. Goods and parcels continued to be handled at the station but were sent via the Severn & Wye line. The station was at its busiest shortly before its closure, due to the war. The scene, right, shows local enlisted men departing in around 1915, probably bound for Brecon Barracks. Crowds of townsfolk have come out to wave them off.

Nearly six years after closure, the station still looks neat and cared for in this June 1922 view, which makes it all the more surprising passenger facilities were not transferred to it when the S & W station had burnt down in 1918. In the background is the goods shed, saved from demolition in the 1980s at the eleventh hour by local former railwayman Mike Rees and now open as a museum, the only reminder left today of Coleford's railways.

Perhaps the most famous passenger to ever use the station was the composer Sir Edward Elgar, whose brother lived at Ellwood. When visiting, he required a horse and cart to be awaiting his arrival because of the amount of luggage he brought with him. One senior Colefordian remembers as a youngster being patted on the head by the great man when he helped to load it all. The view on the right shows a train coming up from Whitecliff Quarry in 1965. Today this bridge has gone and the cutting beyond is occupied by the council's new offices.

The chimneys of Whitecliff House can just be seen in front of Newland Street bridge, which still stands today and which carried the branch from Whitecliff Quarry into Coleford. The railway was intended to take advantage of the Forest's natural resources of coal, iron ore and timber. Local council development proposals after WW2 envisaged its reopening to provide a more direct route to South Wales but it was never a realistic possibility. When the main line between Bristol and London was up graded in the 1960s in preparation for high speed trains, large quantities of stone ballast were conveyed from Whitecliff Quarry (seen below) for onward transit, via Gloucester. The line carried more tonnage than at any other time during its history, just before it closed. The quarry is still in operation today but its entire output now leaves by road – surely the railway would have been a better option than the narrow roads in this part of Dean.

The first iron rails to reach Coleford were actually the plates of the Monmouth Tramroad, opened in 1812. It ran from a junction with the S & W Tramroad at Howler's Slade down to Monmouth. It had largely fallen out of use by the time the Coleford branch was built on much of its route in the 1880s. The picture above was taken in 1950 and shows part of the old trackbed, running between the houses and through the centre of Coleford.

A general view of Whitecliff around 1900. The large house just to the left of the road in the centre distance is Lower Whitecliffe Farm house, which was demolished circa 1910. Nearer, on the right just past the white painted cottage, is the old Pound, where stray animals were kept.

Many of the areas roads were built in the 19th century under the auspices of the Dean Forest Turnpike Trust, who established turnpike houses and gates at various points to collect the tolls. Coleford, being at the centre of a hub of radiating routes, had several – at Poolway, Coalway Lane End, Whitecliff, Scatterford, Crossways, Sling, Staunton and Berry Hill. They were abolished on 31 December 1888 and the newly formed local council took over responsibility for the roads. This photograph of Poolway Turnpike House was taken on that final day. Uriah and Harriet Blanch were the last resident toll collectors, and members of the family and passers-by pose for photographer John Porter. The house was subsequently purchased by Isaiah Trotter but has since been demolished.

This imposing police station was built in 1860 on the corner of Gloucester Road and Lord's Hill, replacing an earlier station just across from it at No. 3 Gloucester Road. It was the home for the Inspector and Sergeant and their families, besides being a police station. Courts were held fortnightly. If you had the misfortune to attend the locals said that you were 'Up the Steps'. It was demolished in 1964 following completion of the new police station and magistrate's court on the site of Bank House, just visible behind. This photograph of it was taken about 1905. A division of Mounted Police were stationed here during the 1926 General Strike.Note the letterbox in the wall, the gas lamp and the milestone behind it, engraved '9 miles to Severn Bridge'. It refers to the now demolished railway bridge. From 1889 the streets were lit every night, except at full moon, for 8 months of the year for which the Parish was charged £80, per annum by the local gas company. This would have necessitated the services of a man employed as a lamp lighter. Opposite the old police station, at the bottom of Lord's Hill, stood the Coleford Corn Warehouse of J. T. Adams, corn and flour merchants. Nearby a Mr Brookfield sold paraffin. Two shire horses drew the large paraffin delivery tank, which was mounted on a wagon. Bank House, just peeping out from behind the police station, was the home of a brave Colefordian, Angus Buchanan. Born in 1874, he was awarded the Victoria Cross during the First World War in 1916 but was wounded shortly afterwards, resulting in blindness. He relinquished his commission and returned to Oxford University, obtaining a degree in Law, qualified as a solicitor and followed this profession in Coleford. He died in 1944. In 1919, in honour of Captain Buchanan's gallantry, some land was purchased by public subscription on the west side of the town to form a memorial park, complete with children's rides, sports facilities and a shelter. It was administered by a committee and maintained largely by volunteers. The postcard on the right relates to a meeting of the Memorial Trustees and was posted in 1931.

THE ANGUS BUCHANAN V.C. MEMORIAL.

Date as Postmark. *13, HIGH NASH, COLEFORD.*

Dear Sir/

The Monthly Meeting of Trustees and Committee of the above Memorial will be held at the Forester Coffee Tavern, Coleford, on Monday June 8 *at* 7 *p.m., when your attendance is requested.*

Yours faithfully,

GEO. T. HARPER, Hon. Sec.

AGENDA:

General

The Post Office was originally in Newland Street but around 1900 it moved into premises in the High Street. This postcard view was posted in July 1903, the sender remarking '*Its lovely in Coleford this evening*'. Note the Queen Victoria 'VR' post box on the right. The Postmaster, who lived on the premises, stands in the doorway and a telegram boy, in his smart uniform, by the window. Girls also undertook the responsible work of delivering telegrams too, occasionally to inaccessible places such as Staunton iron mine, where one intrepid female recalled being lowered into the workings, delivering in person to the recipient in case an urgent reply was required. Miss Fyffe's stewardship as Postmistress is still remembered with affection by local people, whilst the last post left for Lydney at 7.30 in the evening. The office in High Street continued to be used until about 1968 when it was rebuilt. The new building remained in use until 1998 when the Counter Services were moved to a shop nearby.

Originally a house, this early 19th century property became a hotel around 1908. Advertised for families and commercial travellers, it was also another Temperance hotel. The Temperance movement often found great favour in industrial and mining areas such as the Dean, where drunkeness was rife amongst working men. This postcard advertising the hotel was actually sent by proprietor G. Horwood in 1910. The golf links referred to is the then course at High Nash, which has since been built upon. The single storey annexe was later used briefly as a private school and the whole of the property is now owned by the Forest of Dean District Council.

Braceland House, near Christchurch, was built in the first half of the 19th century, mostly of stone recovered from the demolition of Highmeadow House, Lord Gage's old mansion near Newland. In 1938 the grounds surrounding the house became the first Forestry Commission campsite to be opened in Britain and it remains a popular spot with visitors and campers today.

The Mount of Olives Pentecostal Church at Poolway, which was designed and built by the Broadwell-based company of Gibbard & Jenkins Ltd. Members of the Assembly of God denomination first arrived in Coleford just after WW2, when the Carter factory manufacturing 'Ribena' relocated to the town. They originally met in a wooden building at Cinder Hill, until funds were raised to build this church in 1960. A hall was added in 1965. The illuminated cross on the front of the church can be seen from some distance away at night.

St. Margaret Mary's Church and the Priest's house were built in 1933, this view being taken shortly after. The first Roman Catholic services were held at No. 4 Newland Street in 1930, with two nuns in residence (now Fowlers, the ironmongers). George Badman, a local catholic businessman, brought Father Towne, parish Priest at Monmouth to say the first Mass in the Forest. The Clifton diocese took exception to a priest being brought in from the Cardiff diocese and quickly installed their own priest, Fr. Andrew Waters, who took over the house at No. 4, the nuns being sent back to Monmouth.

Looking down Boxbush Road in the early 1930s, towards the Congregational Independent Chapel. The small shed like building with the white roof, halfway up the hill, was Ernie Martin's monumental masons workshop (demolished in the 1980s). Salter & Son, tailors, had their premises on the corner.

A close up study of the Independent Chapel in Staunton Road, circa 1910. During WW2 volunteers spent many hours in here bottling locally grown fruit and making jam to help with the food shortages. The building date 1842 is prominently displayed on the projecting Doric porch with two columns. The chapel became the United Reformed Church in 1972 when the Presbyterians and Congregationalists joined together but has since closed and been converted to apartments. The Rudge family lived in the house next to the chapel for many years, Mr Rudge being a clerk in Lloyds Bank. Later Mr A. O. Marshall, a dentist, had a practise at the house.

View from Boxbush Road of St. John the Evangelist Parish Church, about 1910. It is a fine spacious building with chancel and transepts by S. Gambier-Parry. Sir Charles Nicholson carved the oak reredos as a 1914-1918 War Memorial. There is a 20th century oak lectern and carved stone chancel screen, appropriate as products of the Forest. When they were intending to replace the church on the Tump, the Church Commissioners acquired land in the vicinity of where the Council Offices now stand. Before a new church could be built the railway was proposed and it took precedence. The new Anglican place of worship was subsequently built on the other side of town in 1880. The picture below right, is a rare late 1870s view of how St. John's church, designed by the architect F.S. Waller, was intended to be. With money running short, certain parts of it such as the south transept and porch were added later but the tower, at a projected cost of £2,500, was never built. It would have made quite a difference to Coleford's skyline. The Old Vicarage, below left, is late 18th century with 19th century extensions, having been built originally to serve the 15th century Anglican chapel on the Tump, demolished in 1820 to make way for the octagonal church which St. John's replaced. The ivy clad building is seen here in a view circa 1905 by John Porter. This vicarage served St. John's church until 1970.

ST. JOHN.—COLEFORD NEW CHURCH.
PHOTOGRAPHED BY W. HARDING WARNER.

Coleford Church Choir, 1940. Back row, l-r: Sidney Byard, Charles Saunders (manager, Lloyds Bank), Bob Adams (owned a decorating business), Harry Rosser, Thomas Joseph, Edward Wilce, Albert Edmunds, George Butler (tenor soloist), Kenneth Adams. Third row: Mrs Olive Gwilliam (organist), Peggy Dangerfield (father was an Inspector at the Blue Bus office), Evelyn Adams, Betty Edey, Miss Ethel Cole (Head of St. Johns School), Josie Gallop, Miss Martin, Miss Winifred Canter (Head of Broadwell School), Ursula Phipps (now Mrs Smith), Agnes Hughes (now Mrs Poulton). Second row: Unknown, Michael or Cyril Hodges, Unknown, Vivian Morris, Rev. Lawrence Wraith (Vicar 1938-47. Moved to Yate. Known to many children as Uncle Lawrence), Maurice Driver, ? Smart, Norman Smith. Front row: ? Smart, David Ellis (lived at the Scowles), Unknown, Unknown, Gilbert Peters (errand boy at White & Miller, butchers. He subsequently took over the business, now run by his wife and son), Raymond Bullock.

Victoria Road in about 1950, looking very much the same as it is today but for the lack of parked cars and television aerials. At the far end are the gates to the Memorial Recreation Ground, dedicated to the memory of Captain Angus Buchanan VC. Mr Hinton made the gateposts. One was erected the wrong way round and remains so to this day, although the gates were refurbished in the 1990s. The Duchess of Beaufort performed the ceremonial opening of the new gates in 1935.

Like the other main Forest towns, Coleford has always been surrounded by industrial concerns and works, although these have changed over the years. The arrival of H. W. Carter's from Bristol in 1948, to a new purpose built factory at the top of the town at High Nash, brought the manufacture of the internationally known 'Ribena' drink to Coleford. Subsequently bought by Beecham's Ltd, the factory continues in operation today under the auspices of the Smith Kline Beecham group, employing a workforce of 500 in the 1970s. The complex has grown into one of the largest and most modern in Europe, for the production of fruit drinks in Tetra Pak cartons and plastic bottles, and the factory's capacity is still increasing. The advert on the left, with the factory in the background, is from 1960.

Quarrying in the Dean has become an emotive issue of late, with many believing that the Forest should be left as an area of undisturbed, sylvan beauty. However, it has always been a working forest, being colonised largely by miners and ironworkers in the first place, and there are many more who believe that this is the status quo which should be maintained. The view on the right shows Stowfield Quarry, just outside the town, in about 1960.

Boilermaking at Fred Watkin's works at Sling, near Coleford, has ceased in the last few years and the company now concentrates on heavy haulage operations. This view, also from around 1960, shows a consignment of new boilers about to leave. The company also had interests in quarrying, brick making, land development, civil engineering, and plant and crane hire.

For many years the town held a regular carnival and there were often visiting entertainments to amuse the local population too. The photograph above shows a group of musical clowns dressed for one of the carnivals before WW1, whilst in the bottom view the Circus comes to Coleford in 1905. There is a team of six horses in harness, hauling the publicity wagon around the town to drum up business. Presumably, they were normally required to pull the 'Big Top' and equipment? The photograph on the right was taken at Coleford Fair – always held on the 20 and 21 of June – in 1952.

The Coombs, at Sparrow Hill on the northern outskirts of the town, was completed in 1860, its building being commissioned by wealthy local resident Isaiah Trotter, who subsequently lived there until his death in 1906. Charles Searle, the London-based architect who designed it, also designed the Baptist Church in Newland Street. Today, The Coombs is a residential and nursing home.

Trotter's fortune was acquired partly as a result of his own business acumen – he was a maltster and corn merchant – and partly from bequests. He was a Baptist and took an active part in the town's life, also being known as a great benefactor. One of his legacies is the row of ten almshouses at The Gorse, built in 1889 in memory of his wife Jane and which he subsequently conveyed to the Baptist Church.

Bibliography and sources

Coleford. The History of a West Gloucestershire Forest Town — Dr. Cyril Hart. 1983
The Victoria County History Gloucester, Vol V. The Forest of Dean — Ed. by N. Herbert. 1996
The Great Western Railway in Dean — H.W. Paar. 1965
The Wye Valley Railway and the Coleford Branch — B.M. Handley & R. Dingwall. 1998
Coleford's Churches — Harold S. Bright

June Anne Webb is Chairman of the Coleford and District WI Country Market.
Keith Lloyd Webb BEM. JP. is an Inclosure Commissioner for the Forest of Dean.